Voluptuous Gloom

Also by Oren Wagner

The Last Redcoat (2006)
My Life in the Former Colonies (2007)
I Heard You Twice the First Time (2008)*

*(Harder to find than a Taliban keg party)

Voluptuous Gloom

Oren Wagner

The New York Quarterly Foundation, Inc.
New York, New York

NYQ Books™ is an imprint of The New York Quarterly Foundation, Inc.

The New York Quarterly Foundation, Inc.
P. O. Box 2015
Old Chelsea Station
New York, NY 10113

www.nyqbooks.org

Copyright © 2009 by Oren Wagner

All rights reserved. No part of this book may be used or reproduced in any manner whatsoever without written permission of the author. This book is a work of fiction. Any references to historical events, real people or real locales are used fictitiously. Other names, characters, places, and incidents are products of the author's imagination, and any resemblance to actual events or locales or persons, living or dead, is entirely coincidental.

Some of these poems have appeared in *Zen Baby*, *Re:mark*, *New York Quarterly*, *Poesy*, *Fuck!*, *Alpha Beat Press*, *The Inquisition Poetry*, and *Free Verse*. Also some poems appeared in a broadside by Platonic 3Way Press, a broadside by Strong heArt Press of Yellow Springs, Ohio, and a slender collection of poems by Ego Creek Press.

First Edition

Set in New Baskerville

Layout and Design by Raymond P. Hammond
Additional Editing by Sarah Swiss and Whitney Su

Cover Photography by Doug Earl
Pretty girl with flower—Katie Lyn Coles

Library of Congress Control Number: 2009939407

ISBN: 978-1-935520-19-1

Voluptuous Gloom

Acknowledgments

Special thanks to Tim Landrum, Ashley LaFollette, Don Winter, Davy DeLa Fuente, Diana Juarez, Marcella Riccardi, Paolo Iocca, Karlee Dell, Brian White, Paul Lahr, Al Humphrey, Christina Carter, Heather Allison, and Shannon Anderson. Without you, life would be very vanilla.

Also thank you to Raymond Hammond and everyone at *NYQ*, Joni Earl, Sarah Strong, Sarah Swiss, and my family near and far.

For Steve Henn and the Henn Family

Contents
(by title or first line)

I'll never leave	15
rain on grave markers	16
there is nothing	17
Eve	18
Sunflower	19
even though	20
my heart has a hole the	21
Etiquette	22
Hours/Ours	23
in a dream I	24
paying attention	25
Winifred's Birthday	26
if I could talk to	27
running in the lord's name	28
when you told	29
I'll walk the length	30
Exodus	31
if the future is still	32
if your lungs fail before mine	33
the noise in my head evacuates	34
you know that feeling	35
tonight the moon	36
Hibernation	37
these lead flowers	38
on the phone with you	39
this immaculate heart	40
last night	41
blessed by	42
atmosphere clear	43

dead clock	44
I want to close my eyes for sleep	45
this face	46
Without You	47
November 4th	48
Concrete Eyelids	49
adjectives fall from my mouth	50
it's hard to translate	51
when lips are lost	52
Weightless Repetition	53
late summer storm is so beautiful	54
Fragile	55
Easter Sunday	56
Sunset at Brown County	57
I'm glad to have lived this life	58
things are as they were	59
rain again twelve hours later	60
today my heart is in my throat	61
small amount of humidity	62
the fangs of pain sink	63
Spica	64
we are at our best when we	65
Goodnight	66
I go to church to feel	67
East of Columbia limestone	68
Meteorology	69
Living Buddha	70
I hold your memory	71
I remember your face	72

The union army marches	73
you put lightening bolts in my heart	74
Modern Votive	75
August 27th, 2:28 Central Time	76
Mind Tricks	77
I construct a brand new interior	78
Harmony	79
Eve II	80
Luna	81
When the last spell is cast	82
Christmas Day	83
Death in the Family	84
I think about you all the time	85
Dead Letter Office	86
Living Christ	87
My heart doesn't fill up	88
Green Wedding	89
I sail your ocean bones	90
Ferris Wheel	91
Tin Star	92
outstanding	93
a beautiful sunset	94
gripped in grief	95
Mantra	96
I feel a little crazy on the day's intake of medication	97
Inaudible Voices	98
Saint Francis	99
The Colony of Your Heart	100
Within	101

Electric Fence Jumping	102
Let Me Tell You Honey	103
Lilly	104
530 AM	105
New Dark Age	106
crossing the desolate	107
Three	108
Voluptuous Gloom	109
tomorrow I come undone	110
Fifth Birthday Present	112
Rail Trail	113
this spring of emotion	114
3/30	116
sitting in the back seat of your friend's car	117
The Moon Over Nye, Montana	118
again my mind turns to you	120
Un-American Prayer	123

*"If you raise a glass to love you've passed,
won't you raise a glass to me..."*

—*Royston Langdon*

I'll never leave
even when the levee
breaks
I'll learn to swim

rain on grave markers
evaporates
when the sun comes
out of hiding

there is nothing
like reading sad German
poetry when you're
already feeling
emotionally unstable

Eve

when I have
all the sweet
fruit in existence
I'll still choose
your red apple

Sunflower

sunflowers bow their heads
like they are mourning
the loss of their dearest family member

even though
you are not near
I take great refuge
in knowing we share
the same earth

my heart has a hole the
size of the Williamsburg Bridge
at the thought of you
leaving

Etiquette

I don't know how to act in public
just ask all of my ex-girlfriends
and former employers

Hours/Ours

the sound of ten thousand
clocks winding down
the sound of one
heart beating
then another

in a dream I
tied birds to your
dead limbs
to animate you
again

nothing
seemed out of place

paying attention
to the gravity
in my voice
sunk like the
USS Indianapolis
in the ocean of
my sad vernacular

Winifred's Birthday

I love you
all 68 years worth of you
I hope the geese on your pond
honk the birthday song for you

if I could talk to
you openly about my
problems, I'd have no
problems
all I need is you
the unconditional
ear to bend

running in the lord's name
but there is no lord
no heaven to run to
all my youth has been
euthanized, my enthusiasm
evaporated

when you told
me you were engaged
I felt disengaged
from the world
for a month,
being aloof
is my way of saying
congratulations

I'll walk the length
of the Oregon Trail
to be with you
to see your eyes
and embrace you
in my existence
one more time

Exodus

wandering the desert
with Stars of David in
your eyes
commandments rain down
like manna

do this
don't do that

forty years worth
of wrong turns

if the future is still
and I am here
I pray you'll be there too
to share something beautiful

it's paradise in every breath
kingdom-come within

if your lungs fail before mine
I'll continue to breathe for you
if your heart stops first
I'll trade my heart
that has carried you all this time

the noise in my head evacuates
so I can pay attention to your
romance language
coffee eyes open to study the
dull dead lights

together
we learn
luminosity

you know that feeling
when you look inside
your full closet and think
you don't have anything to wear?
that's how I feel
about everything
currently
in my life

tonight the moon
has a halo that shines
its light down
I'm over here in Indiana
missing you
hoping the lunar beams
fill your eyes
hoping you think of me too

Hibernation

I'm distracted with
thoughts of you
I can't work
sleep
eat
drive my car
without
distractions
I want to
cool your waters
kiss your feet
sleep until
spring
next to you

these lead flowers
we carry between us
transmute to
real flesh organisms
in our nearness
with fragrance and
colour
soft to the touch

perishable

these petals turn
back to metal
when we are apart

on the phone with you
near the end of the call
there are no words spoken on
either side
outside the crickets are
speaking their little
cricket minds
while two humans struggle
to say goodnight

this immaculate heart
beats to what she thinks
is important

it's all perception

this morning precipitation
fell while I was asleep
occasional thunder woke me
I felt my heart beat too
all ventricles
repeating its mantra

last night
and the night before
I had dreams starring you
I woke up missing you
even though you are still near
you are part of everyone I see
part of me
this feeling makes omnipresence
seem believable

blessed by
you twice
in different
dreams last
night. one
I held
your cold
hand while
we walked
through my
hometown the
second we
were married
now I
wish I
were still
asleep instead
of writing
this poem

atmosphere clear
auras circle the living
Buddha molecules fill the lungs
each breath in
you're in love
each breath out
northern lights for eyes
lambs instead of teeth in your smile
this ambient heaven
you put me in

dead clock
above the stairwell
I moved its arms
so it will always read
8 o'clock
its cadence has long been
silent
my lungs move up
and down instead

the sound of my feet
tick on the steps
fourteen times

I want to close my eyes for sleep
and wake up next to you
everyday
I want to dance to music uncomposed
and speak in a language unwritten
I want to break the arms of time
and stay young forever with you

this face
I carry in memory
these lava bones
these fingers of aluminum
this summer night I'm not alone
these heavy rain clouds
these empty streets
this primary colour I drown myself in
these storefront windows
these forgotten lights
this body song
this bossanova

Without You

what would I be without you?
a painting without a cave
a language without articulation
a kiss without sensation
a colour wheel minus the colour blue

the world would undoubtedly
erode to nothing and the eons
pass away
before I'd learn a single thing
about anything

November 4th

I'm surrounded by things that glow
and things that don't
your calcium kiss is still
on my mouth
august is november
and your side of the bed is cold
the concrete I lay on while on the phone
is cold
cigarettes and waxing moons
glow

I don't

Concrete Eyelids

sink to the bottom of a dream filled night
darkness wraps around like a placenta
I am born again with the rising sun
I live an entire lifetime in one day
middle and old age decline with the zenith
to dusk
to the inevitable shadows that follow

adjectives fall from my mouth
when I talk about
you

lonely
cold
beautiful

I want to take you into my
arms and make you mine
but you are distant
you are light
millions of miles from here
bright enough for me to see
but certainly not close enough to feel

it's hard to translate
hurt into
language
grapes of wrath
squeezed into
wine
it's nothing sacramental
or special

body fills up
with white noise
the mind is black

the sky falls out of place
in the same way
gravity affects
an hourglass
the same way
heavy rain beads
down the windshield

when lips are lost
and international
tongues have brightened
the kind that burn
on top of your head
and lick your halo
to world's end
to killing the dead
when urges stop feeling urgent
and "do not disturb" signs
hang from the doorknob
of your soul
then
feeling alone
feels like being together

Weightless Repetition

the dust settles
we all settle dust to dust
teeth will unclench
fists will come undone
the bitter sweet will be neither
bitter nor sweet
the tired Gospels close
all the testaments accounted for
old and new
the entire world can be paraphrased
in the repetition of the cricket noise
outside my bedroom window

late summer storm is so beautiful
lightening flashes every five seconds
the rumble of thunder felt
deep in my chest
the streets are undrivable
so I sit in my parked car and
wonder what you are doing at this
moment?
it only rains like this
in Indiana
sitting still is what I'm doing
at this moment

Fragile

I left the house
only to buy eggs
I've been gone
four hours
right foot feeling
heavy on the
speed pedal
it's hard to see
the road through
the tears

I have no idea
where I am
but I feel compelled
to drive on
thinking there will
be better deals on
breakfast foods
somewhere up the road

Easter Sunday

I should program the caller I.D.
on my phone to read
"he beat you"
so I feel less sorry
about not answering calls
from my dad
he's just going to try and guilt trip
me into doing something for him
and he's never done anything for me
in this life except teach me how to be
an asshole

Sunset at Brown County

the cold of spring
watching the sun set
behind the trees
a gray haze fills
the sky around
I'm cold enough to
want my jacket
but I don't want
to walk back to the car
and leave your side for
those couple minutes
we stayed well after
the sun was gone
well after a deep chill
entered our bones

I'm glad to have lived this life
to have a chance to know you
to learn from you
to love you
to worry about you
to be worried about
to take you into my arms like family
to listen to the words you speak
to sleep at night knowing you'd call
down the angels of heaven to
watch over me

things are as they were
waiting for the sky to fall
what are colours without eyes?
listening to distant voices then
the wind takes over
I'm waiting for the days to pass
learning the language of numbers
counting the grains of sand in
an hourglass
there is a finite number
I see the future
there will be darkness and dust

rain again twelve hours later
thunder scares the dog
the uncertain scares me
not dying but
the stuff that happens
in the meantime
a five-year-old version of me
would hide under the bed
until the storm had passed
the 31-year-old version
stares out the window at
the bending trees
and the impromptu river
in my driveway

today my heart is in my throat
constricted swallowing
back and forth between bad
and not so bad
heart, I tell you not to split
things will be fine before long
there will be a ticker-tape-parade
and floats and giant balloons shaped
like my favourite cartoon characters
all in my honour
all when this heart feels love again

small amount of humidity
filled the air
us
with our backs on the
footbridge over
the creek
staring up through the
trees
the moon to the left

the past and future
are nowhere at this moment

our laughter splits
through the night and
darkness that
envelops us

talking sweet about nothing
until the tiredness of
3 a.m.
beacons us home

the fangs of pain sink
into my heart
I know I'll never know
your love

at the edge of town is
a woods that invites
me in to be lonely
together
tree limbs are still
bare, late winter wind
cuts through my clothes
my own skin isn't
enough to embrace me
this is a feeling I will
never get used to

Spica

I pull your
heaven from the sky
one ion at a time
all twenty eight billion light-years
condensed
folded
born again
it's the second big bang
from the beginning of the universe
to this hour we sit
doing nothing
we pull heaven from the sky
in the black hole of our ignorance
our single beauty
the event horizon of true love

we are at our best when we
are full of regret
future fossils
waiting for the earth
to cover us
cradle robber
winds of trade from the
black market
I listen to you like you are
a burning bush
you bring my city to rubble

days later we are christmas shopping
for the future dead
we'll clean their attics and find our
unused presents

Goodnight

to the wind blowing my Japanese
wind chimes outside
to the month belonging to Capricorn
eyelids are heavy as sleeplessness turns the channel
turns the pages turns over in bed
to my reflection on the television screen
to my girlfriend's legs sticking out of the covers
to your multicoloured ink tattooed on your ribs
and to every wave on your rib cage ocean, goodnight

I go to church to feel
closer to you
you give my mind sanctuary
my presence in this building I
am metaphysically capable of
holding your body close to mine
inside these walls we are one

I take your sacred heart
and make it my own
I take your breath and
animate the rest of my life
this solitary communion
reminds me I am not
alone

East of Columbia limestone
tries to reconstitute itself
into the ocean-floor
the highway cuts into
your landscape
it's easy to see how
the past has no memory
humans come along and
create history
and spoil everything with
their language
but before *us*
was *this*
was indescribable
unarticulated beauty
that can only
be actualized
when nature's selection
seems natural again
when words are suspended
indefinitely

Meteorology

bad weather makes me think of you
inclement, snowed in, stay at home
you are on my mind
and in my mind it is Christmas Eve in
North Manchester all over again
the van can't get out
of the driveway
we are stranded
but at least we have
each other
and enough coffee and
food to last for weeks
and free cable TV
we can't go wrong

Living Buddha

in your smile
I find nirvana
in your voice
I find peace

you would allow
yourself to be devoured
by lions to protect me

with my shadow I am
never alone
autumn leaves float
down the stream
and nothing stays the same
if love lasts as long
as the stars shine
this will be long enough
this light will be light again
a rebirth of religious proportions

I hold your memory
when I lay in bed at night
wondering when I'll see you again?
when I'll watch another sunset with you?

I hold your memory
when I drive to nowhere
listening to music I think you'd
like to be listening to
raindrops bead together on the waxed windshield
there is something beautiful in the
patterns the weather makes
there is something beautiful in everything

I remember your face
only in various
flashes of memory
but I'm glad I remember
if I carry you for the rest of
my days only as a memory
then that's ok

if your metal ever cuts
my hand
and my blood litters
your floor
leave the stains as a
reminder that I was alive there
casting my shadow there
breathing in and out there
looking at your face

The union army marches
to the song of courtship
Crossing the high-plains
thinking of the Holy Roman Empire
Suspended time zones
everywhere feels like home
Stars of David super nova
when I remember your eyes

DNA comes undone
in this beautiful moment
This is something better than love
You can't seem to put your finger on it
But you know I'm right
You feel it in your bones

you put lightening bolts in my heart
and fill my eyes with stars that aren't made of light
you are beautiful beyond my imagination
your confetti skin touches the party of my flesh
and this I love
when eleven at night becomes two the next morning
but we are one
one entire entity
twenty fingers locked
unable to tell the difference between
mine and
yours
unable to articulate our own understanding

Modern Votive

I drove past the place where you died
silenced the radio and gave a tap to my brake
the rear-view mirror I stared into a half mile down
the road. The whole time

with you in mind.

I pulled into my driveway
surrounded by nightfall
unlocked the front door of the house
and left the porch light on for you

August 27th, 2:28 Central Time

I'll be there when I can't
with the in breath, I'm at your side
the moon over you, I'll be watching too
the earth below, you'll be standing on me
anything with true emotion
right beside you
I will gladly take your fear and pain
as my own, like Atlas carries the world,
in this lifetime and beyond
wherever the wind is strong enough
to move the leaves
there I am moving also

Mind Tricks

it's odd how
a door creaking open
sounds like the voice
of a former lover
whispering your name
or a cloud in the sky
looks exactly like
Bullwinkle
or the dead
calico cat
in the middle of
Michigan Road
upon closer proximity in my car
is nothing more than
a small cardboard box
the mind is always looking
for patterns and meaning
form and reason
inside the reasonless
and meaningless

I construct a brand new interior
it is not a sequel
if I could render this life around you
I would combine our spaces
the moon would shine down
bright enough to
cancel this darkness
you exist in binary blips
mobile and cellular
two dimensional and four
my head feels fucked
and completely reasonable all at once
you are various
I am more than transformation
we are corresponding elements
we are superimposed

Harmony

there is harmony
in the leaves that have fallen
over the eons
from constellations frail

this gloomy earth,
with its destroyed seasons
and imaginary solstice and unimaginable equinox,
is a bright enough star
for someone who is looking at it from the appropriate
distance

I say a word like serenity
and lack the language
to justly describe it
other times I say words like annihilate
and know their alphabet
all too well

Eve II

after the apple
we knew it would be
a matter of time before
the Great Animator
evicted us from our home
watching our last sunset
in Eden she turns to me
and says, "Today didn't
exist yesterday"
this from the woman
I love, my own, made from
my flesh, my own rib
the woman who would
labour through Cain's birth
I say, "Tomorrow we have
the pain of the world to share"

Luna

man lands on an unkempt
moon. craters and dust
I can't believe this
untidy heavenly body
controls the tides!

many small steps have
been made, but have
they been in the
right direction?
here is another full moon,

on the eleventh day of a
month passing away into
the next. other bodies are
like jack-o'-lanterns in
the sky, passing away

the moon will wane into
something new, something
borrowed, something blue
giant leaps into the
future. a future of

craters and dust

When the last spell is cast
and the final shell-shocked
we all laugh until our sides split
and our stitches will be removed
I'm living with your ghost
it haunts these lonely nights
my Doppler ears turned on
hearing what you can't

the time of night before the dawn
drowns out the noise
my pregnant mouth giving birth
to triplets again
rejuvenated resurrected reincarnated
emotionally bound together
the greatest emptiness ever felt
slowly being filled

Christmas Day

sugar melts
this wooden tongue
an advance of the dharma mind
this wooden tongue
repeats the mantra
of sweet termite thoughts and carpenter nails
repeats the mantra of a climbing honeysuckle vine
the woodbine and the dark possibilities of samsara

sugar melts
these snow capped eyes
that meditate on time and movement
half open half closed
meditating on the winter birds of Pittsburgh
meditating on the future and knowing
I won't be a part of yours

Death in the Family

hearse driver eating junk food
outside the Mortuary
what an ugly word
he can't seem to find his lips
to sew them close
all the vowels hide behind
an alphabet of yellow teeth
inside the funeral parlor
brother makes a scene
literally doing cart wheels
in the aisles because the witch
is dead
undertaker takes no notice to the
family's embarrassment.
speaking in a soft pale voice
father says, "you're gonna get it
when we get home."

I think about you all the time
your arms like a bonsai tree
a thief hangs the same as a saviour
it all blurs into one
shadows swallow the earth
it's our funeral
but before this I want to tell you
my perfect day would be standing in California
with you
watching the sun disappear into the ocean
we can sink along the fault lines
and we can go south into Mexico
  hours later
    a lifetime later

      the sunrise

Dead Letter Office

The cat has my tongue
language fails me every time
your life I want to share
I have no way of saying this
except here on paper
space and time cut between
harder to cross than any mountain
or ocean
somewhere in my eternal west
lays your eternal east
satellites race above our borders
dead letter offices are filled
with ghosts in envelope form
each note saying something
different than the rest
each a different
undeliverable
I love you

Living Christ

in your eyes
I find heaven
in your voice
I find salvation
you'll wear this
crown of thorns
for me

you'll turn saliva
to wine and we'll be
drunk on each other
from the cross I drive
the nails into you myself
one hammer blow at a time
I confess those sins
to be born again
you cure the leprosy
of my mind
you'll resurrect me from
the ground like a phoenix
from the ash
life eternal I believe in
with you

My heart doesn't fill up
like it used to when I think of you
when I kissed your sun burnt skin
there's no pride in memory
like the hundred graveyards we've passed keep
no thoughts
Remembering the past means nothing to me
all personal tragedies swept under the rug
all secrets are locked up
and I threw away the key
today the last heat of dusk hangs in the air
the sun sets in the west
today I am empty
I am fulfilled

Green Wedding

in a letter
you told me about
your wedding
and your green dress
so I'll tell you
in this poem
my mother wore the same
colour on her day
in front of the justice
of the peace
my dad had on a cowboy outfit
I've seen the pictures
a good-looking couple
San Francisco 1967

your marriages
have many similarities
except it took less than
a year for you to realize
the folly of your groom
instead of the 40 years
it took my mom

I sail your ocean bones
your suntanned skin
head west to California
with me
we'll fake our deaths
and chase ghosts of
beat writers in
Big Sur
we'll go to open mics
in Santa Cruz across the
street from the halfway house
we'll read love poems
written in finger ink on
the spine and rib cage
then north to Red Bluff
where we can sit for days
and do nothing
and nothing will be
perfectly acceptable
then south to Mexico
mañana is the beginning of
forever

Ferris Wheel

terrified
together sitting in
a gondola of a Ferris wheel
I wanted to reach out
and grab your hand in mine
we both suffer
incredibly silly, yet painfully
real Ferris wheel phobias
it could be my crippling bouts
of vertigo, but I can't handle
open-air heights
and you, traumatized by your
older brother trying to throw
you over board as a child
jealous of all the attention
this sister was stealing from him
together we triumphed
we won that battle against gravity
but we haven't won the war

Tin Star

tired we spin on an axis
around this tin star
in our part of the
milky way solar system
uttering syllables
of the dead
we spin with our imagined
madness
our imagined sadness
our imagined tetanus and locked jaw

the old cadence of the heart beats
tired blood around my circulatory system
while my eyes darken and my body breaks
charms from the beast
true love lost
small white pinholes in a black sky
alive but utterly dead
praying a prayer
with no answer…
don't go where I can't follow

outstanding
when nothing feels more than enough
a smile from your white teeth
lost body heat
out standing in a night at the end of November
stars behind a blanket of Canadian originating clouds
you remind me of a friend's mom
I remember the way she tucked me in
when I stayed the night with her son.
she died a few years ago of cancer.
I used to confuse her name with a popular
candy bar's name when I was young
it's not Hershey; it's more like Reese's, but not exactly

a beautiful sunset
is happening
at this moment
over Indiana

I wish you were
here to see it
with me

or witness
gravity pull
tears from my eyes
two nights ago

I hope my life is
as beautiful as
either of these moments

a new dirge song
to fill my ears
the dusk
soon to pass
this great moment
soon to pass
as will everything

gripped in grief
feeling the kind of fragile
that renders my own mirror
reflection unrecognizable
weeks go by
not knowing myself

I'll rewrite this sad poem
as I've written it a hundred times
because I still feel the same

dusk is falling
like seeds from a
dead sunflower
cicadas sing back
and forth from
the mature trees in
the neighbourhood

you are not gone
but I already miss you

there is no rational way
I can tell you to stay
to live with me and become
part of my routine
to love me
to be by my side
and enjoy a future that
only exists in my mind

Mantra

all the words I hold
spell your name
you're the Alpha
in the Omega
when my senses
crave grace
I turn to your silence
I repeat your name
in my head like a mantra
and picture your face
like a Buddha in meditation
like a spiritual pharmacist
on medication
I return to this silence
it's thick in the air
I'm high when I should be low
I'm surrounded when I should
be alone
you're the beginning
to my end
the Om
that fills my space
all the love in this life
that's worth feeling
are in the letters
of give and receive

I feel a little crazy on the day's intake of medication
I've got the electric touch
like a latter-day King Midas
the days feel long
and I feel completely incomplete
rain falls over the neon lights
over my apathy
I wear my forgetful face
if/when I make it out of the house my
5 o'clock shadow has turned into
an 8-week shadow
when I fall to my knees
to beg or pray
I fall
hard
but my prayers have no language
except a beginning and end
"Dear Lord...
...Amen"
nothing in between
except the varying amount
of silent time

Inaudible Voices

inaudible voices fill my daymares and distances
a parallel universe of machines
xerox, facsimile, electronic bee hive
I'm in the centre, with the drone of the yellow jacket

cross pollination has created a bruise coloured hyacinth
the smell is beautiful, but it is all detached,
loose, absent

this elaborate gloom will wane when night falls and things quiet
cornfields and fireflies live beneath the same
old constellations that were given names by people long dead
the stars have their horoscopes, but closer to home,
    two lines connect making
      the electronic seem
        very un-electronic

flowers in the field sleep, the queen
and her yellow jacketed subjects slumber as well
this side of the world is truly silent

Saint Francis

a half moon hangs overhead like it was stolen from a
van Gogh painting and accidentally dropped in the sky
and the trees in this forest were borrowed from a
Rilke poem with the intentions of never
returning them

crickets talk their invisible vocabulary, while
lightening bugs speak their luminous vernacular

mosquitoes have their own gospel
all their mosquito wings are making
noises like tiny Howitzer guns
shooting praises to the god that provides sweet
sacramental wine of flesh

everything alive seemingly on
a pilgrimage toward various impossibilities

and here I am
walking the night with Saint Francis watching over me
like the lost animal I've become

The Colony of Your Heart

a candlelight vigil
in the colony of your heart
time washes away like sand
and you're so close to it all

my dull words cut like butter
when I try to find a new way
to say I love you

I'll die with your starlight in my hand
I'll die with your ring on my finger
I'll die with your songs in my throat

my mouth fills up with space
when I realize I'll share everyday with you
until I can't

until your bay of pigs run dry
until your body lays hollow in a hospital room
until we both pass through the eye of the needle

Within

in everything
  I love you
in every song you hear
  I hope you hear my voice
may the wind blow my
  prayers to you
may the moonlight illuminate
  your nights like I would choose to
when the rain hits your face
  is it not my finger tips?
when the sun rises
  are these not my ambitions?

in the abominations of the earth
  I love you
in silence
  when I am mute
when there is no breath
  left in the sails
and the dust has been alchemized
  to flesh and back to dust
in your darkest hour
  in the drought of hope
you'll understand it was a brief eclipse
  you'll understand there has always
been a light within

Electric Fence Jumping

black and white all over red
an Indian name for an Indian summer
going down hill for the sake of not being able to go up
this life hangs on to the dead
this life hangs on to the well polished
time is a circle, not a straight line
the afterlife is useless in the hands of the dumb
follow the setting sun to the new place you're sure to love
you'll find me in the shadows
you'll find me in the scars of a childhood mostly
f   o   r   g   o   t   t   e   n
we forfeit the past for a version that is more preferable
we lie to ourselves and we break all the rules
we nervously breakdown at a leisurely pace

Let Me Tell You Honey

I write with my left hand to feel closer to you
twelve years of nothing to say all being said at once
I think it's important you know that I know
pull this and that from the top shelf to blow rose scented
kisses
dear beatles, dear prudence
slow dancing with my shadow
let me tell you how sweet it is Sugar
when they play our song

let me tell you Honey, I feel hungover when you're close
twelve months of a quick fix getting broken
I know I know it's unimportant when the entire zodiac has
less pull on you and the sky could fall and you wouldn't care
Martha my dear, I'm so tired of line dancing on the fine
line between
the finite and the infinite

Lilly

how your Sunday best outfit
must have rotted
with twenty years of grave dust
covering you

I think of my last prayer I
prayed by your casket before
they placed you in the ground

where is your soul these
decades later?
is there an eternal garden you're
watching over?
is there a way to listen to the
laughter of your great great grandchildren?
is there an antique mall in heaven where
you worry about paying too much
money for things?

I sign my name the same way I did
when I signed the guest book at your wake
I read your King James Bible we took
from your home after you died knowing
your fingers touched these pages
your eyes read these passages

530 AM

pour salt on the wounds
the lord disapproves
shattered fragile egos
inflate and confiscate, the redcoats are coming
serifs on the letter T let me know you're not fooling
this time
skeleton keys are useless to skeletal remains
blond haired girls on roller coasters upside down
make shameless noise when DNA comes undone
there's a pill for everything
smog over my city makes me feel at ease and puts a
song on my lips
infest and confessed
all of my love is used up on myself
questions that will make you blush
indulge in what's free
make small portions of what has already been rationed
accept that you're nothing exceptional
ask anybody, they've all been surveyed
describe your life without me
finally, imagine that you have to

New Dark Age

sits in confused tongue
confessing to no one
the sins of our fathers
when history is no mystery
because it's written on the faces of everyone
in a dead language
it's a new dark age
to call our own
when this destiny manifests
I will call you Queen
tax those already cradled by your sweet taxation
a bountiful colonization outnumbered
only by the stars in the sky

turning on your side counting the
consonants in the 12 zodiac signs
penance for our motherland
living just to stay alive
a renaissance of reconditioning
The Queen saved God
and history is full of sheols
don't think about it in any other way
no shapes, no sharp edges
a flat line—a redrawn border
now everyone can lose the god
    that has long ago lost us

crossing the desolate
in hopes of reaching the immaculate
a star fell from the sky
near horse-thief basin
we all go a long way
on our trip around the solar system
and we end up, in the end
belly up or face down
as one

it's complicated like surgery
that we windup like this
sewn together
it makes my head spin
to think of all the elements
that had to be right
for our paths to cross
and on a day I didn't want
to get out of bed, we met

friendly fire in the sky
last night the world came to an end
the non-historic wounded-knee
and I stand up
I fly like a sparrow
the 21st century turns to dust
the last star has no more light
but we have our own brightness
a beautiful life lived
to have known each other

Three

in the same welfare hospital
my sister and brother
took their only breaths
I was born
and I will live
three times the life for them
and suffer three times the sorrow
baptized in the church
that would have baptized
them, abused by the dad
who would have abused them
loved by the mother who took
it forty years too long
we all share the surname Wagner
forever. these Wagner children
are buried in a pauper cemetery
with three years of pauper
children between them
I visit small graveyards
and leave tokens on the tombstones
of children without families
the only thing cradling their memory
is a plate in the ground
with its weather eroded alphabet
spelling a dead name
six feet of dirt separating
them and us
and sooner than we'd like to imagine
we will join them in the rows
of cold stone or scattered ash
gone and forgotten

Voluptuous Gloom

take the tick/tock of the clock and replace it with was/is
take this heat away from what I know to be cold
take this sorrow that has found residence in me
take this taste from my mouth when you trade me tongues
take the knots off the loose ends of the have nots
take the centre of your known universe and leave it, like
the neighbourhood cat leaves bird corpses on my doorstep
take my last metaphor and find the sentiment I meant to convey
take the poems I write and know I wrote them for you
take the sleep from your eyes and use them to stare into the
wild night until the stars drop from the sky

give me back to this earth
the dust to dust
the iron and carbon
the blood that spills
the perishing lotus of optimism and skepticism
give me back to this earth using
the simple alphabet we use to archive and
articulate the decay of all that was/is

tomorrow I come undone
tomorrow the caged bird flies/
dies
tomorrow a full lung sigh
tomorrow heaven will evaporate
entire constellations expire
tomorrow Empire States and Sears
Towers will take their place in the sky
a John Hancock zodiac
a Chrysler
Building galaxy
tomorrow brick by brick
a new Tower of Babylon will reach
god's front door
tomorrow a fortune teller looks into an
empty crystal ball
a blank rectangle of paper from
a fortune cookie
tomorrow alphabets will be rewritten
without consonants
AEIOU will have to do
will have to be powerful enough to
convey every message
tomorrow the colour blue disappears
and tiger lilies become the new currency and
the new flag we pledge our allegiance to
tomorrow the kidnapped will be returned
unharmed to open arms
country dirt roads won't seem as dirty
power lines will be replaced by olive branches
New York Times front page will have photos of

artwork instead of murder
columns filled with poetry
the Chicago Tribune will be a tribute to humanity
and humbleness and humility
tomorrow cell phones will be replaced by
smoke signals
crow wings instead of angel wings

Fifth Birthday Present

he couldn't sleep
dinosaurs filled his imagination
if the jurassic plastic figures
weren't being played with
how would they get along
would they know which plastic plants to eat
would they know to stay away from volcanoes
would they understand ken and barbie were not cave
people trying to
kill them

he couldn't sleep
his dinosaurs were not going to make it through the
night without guidance
they were not herbivores or carnivores
they were opportunists
what if they took the opportunity
to eat matchbox cars
the dog's food
or lincoln logs
the game of life would get stuck in their throats
and certainly cause them to choke

he wouldn't sleep
when the house was quiet the boy snuck out of bed
breaking every cardinal law of sleep etiquette
to be with his jurassic plastic figures
and arranged them in perfect
alignment with the dark shadows
of the living room jungle

he was asleep
younger versions of the parents
he'd never get to know
saw the boy lying on the ground
with his fifth birthday present
a Polaroid caught the scene that sat in a shoebox
for the next twenty five years

Rail Trail

walking beside train tracks that haven't hosted
a train for half a century
the rails have been sold for scrap metal
the wooden ties are left in decay
laying in a straight line that goes nowhere
next to the ghost railway is a paved
and well maintained trail folks
use to exercise their out of shape and unmaintained bodies
the excess from many holidays of privilege,
at the end of the trail is a bridge that passes
over Eagle Creek
I sit and listen to the water below and watch
a spider build its web on the chain-linked fence
today children are playing in the creek
about fifty yards away
I can't remember being their age
or at least an age where I would willingly
jump into a muddy stream
I do remember standing on the banks of a river
for a few hours with a fishing pole next
to me that I never cast into the water
I didn't want to feel a live fish die in my hands
I sat there and watched the direction of my shadow
shift along the banks and watched the afternoon
perish into the evening, much like I am doing twenty years later

this spring of emotion
pools onward
in unknown directions
to flood the great plains
of the greatest metaphor
ever constructed
hidden in every drafted line
words spoken endlessly but
rarely actualized into breath
crossing over these wind-burnt lips
the calendar reads August 5th
and as earnestly as I try to make
time stand still it keeps marching on
draining through the event horizon of
the lost
never to be found
the lost love that carries on
westward in her true pioneer fashion
in this flesh we call our own
this exoskeleton keeping the
tired bones in place
this beautiful framework that is never seen
it remembers its fractures and breaks
as your nostrils will remember the
smell of your grandmother's attic
forty years later
the way the muscles around the lungs
know how to laugh or sob
a part of memory that exists
well beyond thought
we suffer the leprosy of great distance

we suffer our own clever design of
a better life
all doctrines and catechisms are
without an ounce of conviction

you
my true love is all I believe in
I write these lines to light the shadow
of my heart
the darkness that collects in regions
of atrophy
the unused finally being useful
finally justifying its space

3/30

second to last day of March
but the weather feels like the 4th of July
minus the fireworks and humidity
the year so far seems void of any fireworks
both physical and metaphysical
I've been working part time a job I dislike most
of the time, the people I work with are alright
most of the public I deal with are alright too
all the same, it's a job I never imagined myself working
the branches of the trees are lifeless and leafless
except for a stray migrating bird that isn't resting
on the power line with the other tired birds
the news is talking about a person being taken off life
support and a co-worker asks if I've been keeping up
with the story, I tell him I have a hard enough time
keeping up with my own family here in Indiana

I'm aware of my own pulse
silent, like a bottle rocket that didn't erupt
and I'm more aware of the passage of time than
I was a decade ago
when day turns to night my eyes aren't fixed
on the horizon
I look instead to the heavenless heavens to find
the thirteenth sign of the Zodiac
which is moving in the form of a lightening storm from
the northwest

sitting in the back seat of your friend's car
you're up front and your friend is driving us somewhere
that we end up not going to because we all decided
that we didn't want to go in the first place
and be surrounded by strangers
the radio is playing INXS
it's the studio version of a song I've only heard
from their live album
and Michael Hutchence sings
"we can live for a thousand years
but if I hurt you I'd make wine from your tears"
your hair is pulled back
and I look at your ear and jaw line
from the back of your friend's Buick
or I look at the passenger side mirror and see your reflection
and the street lights playing off your face
it's at this moment I realize I've developed feelings for you
and I think that anger is a feeling
but I'm not feeling angry
and tired is a feeling and I was feeling tired already
you make me feel another way that I haven't felt in a decade
and if happiness, optimism, understanding and love
were manifested into Arizona, Colorado, New Mexico and Utah
I'd be right there on the border where they all come together
where you can be in four states at the same time
and that's how you make me feel
at 9 at night on the 6th day of September
and every minute since

The Moon Over Nye, Montana

The only living witness to
this setting sun from this reclusive
vantage point, behind these Montana mountains
Yesterday, sleep lives in the west
today I try to capture this moment with my memory
tomorrow all of this will be a new ghost
This is your moon my friend
and I will embrace it with a pen
Venus joins you in the sky
along with a passing dragon shaped cloud
Day-birds give their final song
before the crickets take over the chorus
In front of me the wind is
sweeping the tree tops
To the right a creek is finding
its path of least resistance down
My thoughts turn to you
Your bones are somewhere in China
a small allowance of earth holding them in place
When my soul leaves this body
there will still be the wind swept trees
Tonight I took a moonlit walk
into the valley
A deer startled me in the brush
Fog sneaks in like a
villain to steal the path below my feet
Earth's natural satellite
dips below the mountain
so I point myself back toward
the direction I came from
now I write all 39 lines
by candlelight

The moon has almost completed
an entire cycle since I've seen your lovely face
I pray I will be
laying next to you before it's full again
breathing in and out
in harmony
Our lungs rise and fall like the tides

again my mind turns to you
to take my thoughts away from the dullness
I trace your name onto my skin
circles fill the air like they did in a distant past
and it was in this history I lived on the edge of
a gravel ring
weeks after they lowered you
into the grave
I couldn't remember a single thing about
you except the way you were sprawled
out on your deathbed
a poor huddled mass of paternal flesh
the weight of the world pulling you down
swallowing you in six feet of cemetery dirt
30 years later
aching bones no longer ache
and all the dust has settled on rural roads
when all ends meet at world's end
like the giant sound of one hand clapping
your name repeating in my head since childhood
but never articulated
in the way your name was meant to be spoken
alpha lambda epsilon
the rushing sound of un-dammed water
or the silence of a crypt
or the sound of the last Amen
and when the dreams lift away like
San Francisco fog, I am left chained to a fence
unable to chase after you
and this is the greatest crime to the unimaginable
because I am incapable of action

only witness to the departure
you rise to heaven like the prophet Elijah
I will be completely lost until your light returns to me
until I'm surrounded by your presence
but this feeling is fleeting like crystal breath on a
windowpane
true love passes like a distant cloud and most will
never know its precipitation
or it evaporates on its fall
when there is good news and bad news the
worst of it never balances the best
the fat of the land purges itself away
this is the highpoint of the decline
a split end—fork in the road—a broken wishbone
and the tension it takes to break
hail to the thief
class action and roadside attractions
three p.m. on the 13th of the month
Leo
I pull the thorn out of your foot
I polish your crown
I keep the sun from setting
I call you like your name were Karma
and wait for your response
with ears that focus on nothing
then the anticipation of your voice
and wait for you to return like the parents of an
abducted child wait to see the lost
never losing this vigil
and I hope my breath lasts long enough
that my lungs won't fail before one
mindful in and out breath
or old age doesn't steal my already hazy memory
you'll call my name
an eternal omega
a last flight toward the sun on waxwings
a recited poem in mandarin

the end
then the beginning
the last secret whispered
the last infidel taken down from the cross
the perfect nature of cyclic existence
a straight line to be walked in complete field sobriety
all of the zen babies have been born and lived their lives
and are now zen angels
we are only left with zen
angels
when the Eiffel Tower no longer towers
and the alphabet of Paris has vanished
the last word spoken will be "no"
the last thing heard will be the panic alarm
of all nations
then
and only then
the chorus of heaven
its foreign tongue that gets me every time
the creature of habit teaching the un-learnable
something that cuts deep in the skin
I know the way November sneaks up
soon all that is green will turn brown
the blue sky will turn gray
and seasonal depression will overwhelm
but further from home the universe expands in
the 10,000 directions
a resurrections of a former lifetime
a reoccurring dream

Un-American Prayer

third eye with poor depth perception
thinking about the day ahead of you and the days behind
pucker your lips like you are saying the word breathe
walk down your Denver aisle when the first week of
December has perished
I see the Cape Cod in the tears you're holding back
I feel the Ann Arbor of your kiss
and Chicago of your walk
save your heart
and I'll spill my name in the Atlas of your life

the Apostles and the Apocalypse
the Apache Tribes Men, the assassins and the anarchists know
what time and dimension could never know
the alchemists and the arrogant, the androgynous and the
antichrist know
the pain of the never lasting
that life is fleeting
everything in existence is in a state of decay
recessive genes in the face of your handsome boy
and your world feels out of order
decay
guns drawn and a heart that's bleeding out
decay
the assassin knows the royal flush
the royal sovereign leader, the royal crown cola of
decay
pornography floods your mouth
eyelids blink S.O.S.

how many heartbeats do any of us have left?
can you lift the bent hex of the voodoo eternal?
would you want to?
you have your Rocky Mountain
your mark of the beast
you have all that will be extinct in your hand
it's all yours again and again for the taking
for your greedy hands like Atlanta Braves chopping through
thin air with a tomahawk
or thick air with war spent bullets
or mental breakdowns after 19 years of small town Indiana
walking the railroad tracks to an imaginary friend's house
crying until you taste stomach bile
until your eyes dry
until you stumble over your own two feet and don't
care if you ever stand up from the parallel universe of
railroad ties and steel

if you could earn a living by dying then wealth
would be no problem
a world that carries itself
that travels in an awkward orbit around a sun that
doesn't shine enough
when love doesn't conquer all
when passion cannot be mustered up enough
to hate or detest or deceive
when you just don't care anymore
when your nervous breakdown has broken
the speed of sound
and neighbouring counties can hear your barbaric cries
when you hit the zenith of your decline
when the knots in your stomach have become a noose,
somehow the lead in your heart can still turn to gold
a spark turns into a volcanic eruption
dead letters turn into Braille and you can feel again
things are better than they have ever been,
a decade later the cage bird returns

three decades later Saturn has come and gone
or yesterday the tide takes a sandcastle
yesterday the last candle burns
yesterday the last sacrifice was made
all songs have been sung
and none of this matters
the simple universe spills ahead
take your first step in any direction
even when the destination isn't your destiny
if you're afraid to step into the hedgerow
then you have to go beyond the forest
go beyond yourself

I've been to your home on the range
I've sung the silent night
and I've spent all that you can spend while being homeless
I've grown my hair out for the end of the world that hasn't come
I've bare-ass-mooned the Army tank that sits on the
courthouse square in my crazy town on one of those nights I
swear I was going to die of boredom
and I'd do the same to any other killing machine on display
I've rang salvation's bell, only to be forsaken by the sound
when there's not enough body and blood to go around
and my transgressions are not forgiven
I've stood in a phone booth in the worst of winter for
hours to talk to my first love
I've smoked opium in stranger's living rooms
when the high clears, when the sky has fallen and
 lifted itself back up
I realize I will pass away, these thoughts will pass away
this world will pass beyond nothing

there will be no memory
no recorded history
there will be no Lewis and Clark expedition, there will be no
November 7th 1805, no Apollo Moon Landing, no Berlin Wall,

Dodgers will not have won the 1988 World Series, no Great
Chicago Fire, the Japanese will have never bombed our harbour,
there will be no Jesus or three nails in the cross, no inquisitions,
no statistics, no Alexander Graham Bell, no slaughtering of
Gandhi, Malcolm X, John Lennon, or Martin Luther King,
every killing or birth in future history will be of no
consequence when it is all eroded by the dark winds of time,
when all languages are dead like Latin
tongues and memories will fail and fade
but in the meantime we hold on to life like a spider clings
onto the porcelain of a toilet bowl
because this life is all we have
until the shadows prevail

the dawn is exhumed from last night
the eastern sky is the colour of an autopsy
you'll wake up with last night's tastes in your mouth
roll out of bed and stare into the mirror
concentrating on your beautiful face
I can see something you're not able to notice
the age in your face and you are already falling apart
I love your defections, inflections, your introspections,
when the dead lay themselves to rest we will be there with our
stolen funeral flowers
my only job is to make your pale skin blush
we feel the rush of youth the crush of lost time
everything coming to an end
this beautiful beginning will pass away
but right now the wind is blowing outside these windows
and I am here without you
missing the way you feel
missing your pagan tongue, your binary language
our shared oxygen when we inhale/exhale in our shared nearness
I will be slain by this abandoned feeling
until you are next to me
until you teach me how to say Amen
by never saying a word

photo by Oren Wagner

About the Author

Oren Wagner is the former editor of the small press literary juggernaut *Fight These Bastards* and is a former member of the band Blake/e/e/e. Born in 1977 in Detroit, Michigan, he has lived in Seattle, Washington, Colorado Springs, Colorado, and five various Indiana towns.

About NYQ Books™

NYQ Books™ was established in 2009 as an imprint of The New York Quarterly Foundation, Inc. Its mission is to augment the *New York Quarterly* poetry magazine by providing an additional venue for poets already published in the magazine. A lifelong dream of NYQ's founding editor, William Packard, NYQ Books™ has been made possible by both growing foundation support and new technology that was not available during William Packard's lifetime. We are proud to present these books to you and hope that you will continue to support The New York Quarterly Foundation, Inc. and our poets and that you will enjoy these other titles from NYQ Books™:

Joanna Crispi	*Soldier in the Grass*
Ira Joe Fisher	*Songs from an Earlier Century*
Ted Jonathan	*Bones and Jokes*
Fred Yannantuono	*A Boilermaker for the Lady*
Sanford Fraser	*Tourist*
Grace Zabriskie	*Poems*

Please visit our website for these and other titles:

www.nyqbooks.org

www.ingramcontent.com/pod-product-compliance
Lightning Source LLC
LaVergne TN
LVHW011424080426
835512LV00005B/251